Little KID, BIG City!

New York

WRITTEN by
BETH BECKMAN

ILLUSTRATIONS by
HOLLEY MAHER

QUIRK BOOKS
PHILADELPHIA

FOR MY FAVORITE TRAVEL BUDDY AND EXPLORER.
EXCITED FOR MORE ADVENTURES TOGETHER.

Library of Congress Cataloging in Publication Data
Beckman, Beth, 1980- author. | Maher, Holley, 1987- illustrator.
Little kid, big city! New York / by Beth Beckman ; illustrated by Holley Maher.
Summary: "An illustrated, chooseable-path travel guide to New York City"—Provided by publisher.
LCSH: New York (N.Y.)—Guidebooks—Juvenile literature. |
Children—Travel—New York (State)—New York—Guidebooks—Juvenile literature.
LCC F128.33 .B43 2021 | DDC 917.47/104—dc23
2020036086

ISBN: 978-1-68369-244-7

Printed in China

Typeset in Argone and Wink Wink

Designed by Andie Reid
Production management by John J. McGurk

Quirk Books
215 Church Street
Philadelphia, PA 19106
quirkbooks.com

10 9 8 7 6 5 4 3 2 1

A NOTE BEFORE YOU START YOUR BIG CITY ADVENTURE

With this book, you can explore the sights, tastes, and landmarks of New York City! When you're ready to head to your next destination, look for the options asking where to go next and then turn to the page you chose to visit.

If you want to learn more about a place, turn to the **Adventure Index** in the back of this book for tips and fun facts.

Don't forget the **map**—it's tucked into the very back of this book! You can even tear it out so you can use it as you go.

Are you ready to explore the Big Apple? Let's get started!

NEW YORK, NEW YORK:

such a wonderful town!

There's so much to explore, and so much to be found!

Get ready, get set . . . there's an adventure ahead!

Do you have your map?

Off we go!

We're starting our adventure at the entryway to the city, which has welcomed visitors for centuries!

America's famous First Lady is a symbol of freedom and opportunity.

Standing prominently in New York Harbor, **THE STATUE OF LIBERTY** is the first thing that generations of immigrants would see as they were welcomed to America.

New York City's princess was a gift from France, which built the statue for the United States as a gesture of friendship.

People often wonder why Lady Liberty is green.

Does the color have special meaning?

The Statue of Liberty is coated with a thin layer of copper, which eventually turns a blue-green color due to chemical reactions between metal and water.

A crowning achievement awaits if you can climb the **377 steeeeep steps** through a narrow passage . . . a sweeping view of New York City and beyond from inside the crown.

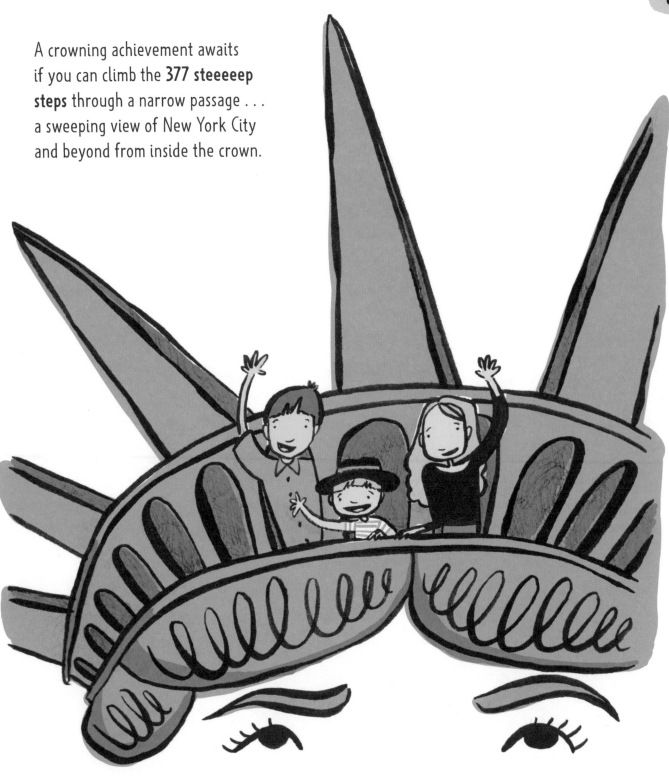

WHERE TO NEXT?

Hungry belly? Turn to page **6**.
Want to see the sights from the water? Turn to page **4**.

A horn blows, passengers rush in— our ferry adventure is about to begin!

The **STATEN ISLAND FERRY** carries millions of people a year across **New York Harbor** to the city's southernmost borough, **Staten Island**. Hop on board and grab a window seat for the five-mile ride—it's free!

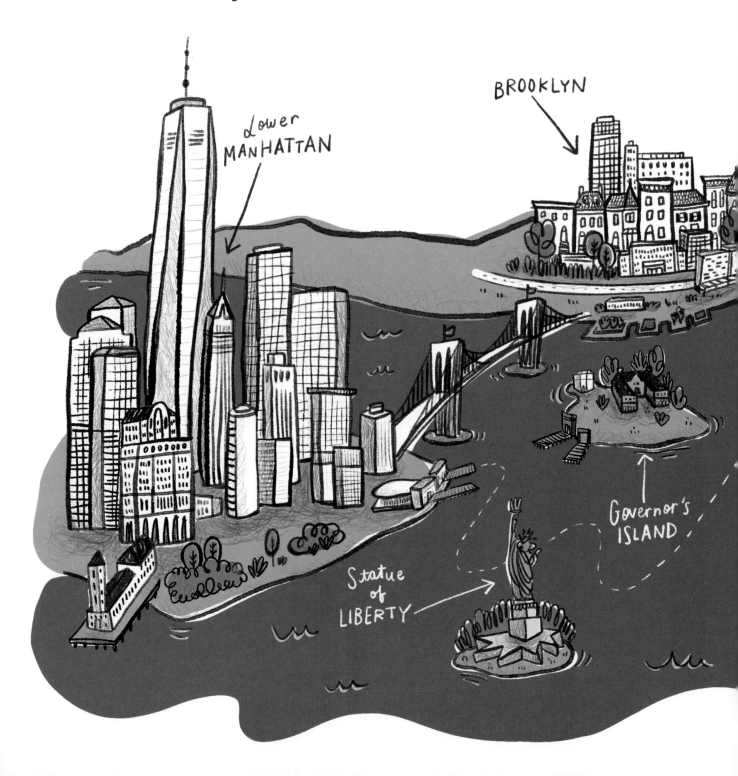

Lower MANHATTAN

BROOKLYN

Governor's ISLAND

Statue of LIBERTY

On Staten Island, you can explore the lush gardens of the **Snug Harbor Cultural Center**. Or stop at the zoo to say hi to **Staten Island Chuck**, the weather-forecasting groundhog who decides if we get six more weeks of winter or spring each year on February 2.

A horn blows again—the ferry is heading back to Manhattan!

WHERE TO NEXT?

Head to your favorite New York City deli! Turn to page **6**.
Walk over the East River! Turn to page **8**.

One toasted bagel, please. And don't forget the yummy cream cheese!

There's nothing better than a bagel from a
NEW YORK CITY DELI:
chewy on the inside, a slightly crispy crust,
and covered in an array of delicious
toppings and schmears.

NYC WATER DEPT.

Do you know what the secret ingredient is?

The water!

That's right—New York City's water has a low concentration of calcium and magnesium, which makes the squishy bread even softer. Other places have tried to re-create New York's bagels, but no one can!

WHERE TO NEXT?

Visit New York's tallest building! Turn to page 10.
Ride horseback through history! Turn to page 12.

Walk this way to cross the **BROOKLYN BRIDGE** by foot and access Brooklyn's waterfront neighborhoods!

Did you know that the Brooklyn Bridge is one of the oldest bridges in the United States? It was finished back in 1883 and was the first steel suspension bridge ever made! It was such an exciting accomplishment when it opened that it was dubbed "the eighth wonder of the world."

The bridge has welcomed lots of famous visitors over the years, including P. T. Barnum and some very large friends of his. Twenty-one elephants walked across the bridge in an opening parade to prove the structure's incredible strength.

WHERE TO NEXT?

Pay tribute in Lower Manhattan. Turn to page 10.
Horse around in Brooklyn! Turn to page 12.

10

A tribute of remembrance can be found on the beautiful **WORLD TRADE CENTER MEMORIAL** grounds.

One World Trade Center overlooks the twin waterfall pools of the **National September 11 Memorial**, which marks the footprint where the Twin Towers once stood. The names of the people who died that day in 2001 are carved into the bronze panels at the edges, and a nearby museum tells about the tragic event.

Today, the tallest building in New York City is the shimmering **One World Trade Center**, which rises even higher than the original Twin Towers that it was built to honor.

WHERE TO NEXT?

Continue exploring by ferry!
Turn to page 20.

Hop on the subway!
Turn to page 21.

DUMBO may sound like the name of an elephant to you, but in New York, it's an acronym for a neighborhood with a bridge view!

DUMBO is home to **Brooklyn Bridge Park**, which offers miles of lush green space and fun playgrounds, right on the waterfront!

DOWN UNDER THE MANHATTAN BRIDGE OVERPASS

No trip to this area would be complete without visiting **JANE'S CAROUSEL**. This antique merry-go-round from 1922 was rescued from ruin and relocated here from Ohio. Today, the horses prance along the river under a glass box shelter. The carousel is considered one of the most beautiful on the planet. Did you ever think you'd be taking in views of Manhattan from horseback?

WHERE TO NEXT?

Fancy a New York slice of cheese? Turn to page page **14**.
Take a ride through New York City's transit history! Turn to page **16**.

Is your hungry belly yelling, "Pizza, please!"?
There's nothing better than a slice of New York City cheese!

There are thousands of **PIZZERIAS** in New York City, but none of them invented the recipe for the famous slice. The original hails from Napoli, a city over 4,000 miles away, in Italy. Italian immigrants brought the recipe to New York and put their own spin on it to create the city's tasty masterpiece: coal-oven baked, thin crust, foldable, and crispy. Perfect every time!

WHERE TO NEXT?

Paddle over to an adventure in Brooklyn! Turn to page 18.

Glide across the water on the ferry! Turn to page 20.

Stand clear of the closing doors—
the **NEW YORK TRANSIT MUSEUM**
is ready to be explored!

COURT ST

COURT

NY TRANSIT MUSEUM

Located underground in an old subway station, the museum showcases the city's subway, bus, and train history. This museum is unlike any other allowing you to step on board a vintage fleet of retired subway cars to see how the world's oldest transit system has changed over the years.

Whoa! Does that train have a ceiling fan? Are those seats made of fabric?

Be sure to look up! The vintage advertisements still remain, featuring many forgotten products that are no longer available today.

WHERE TO NEXT?

Visit Brooklyn's favorite park!

Turn to page 18.

Jump in an (actual!) subway car!

Turn to page 21.

A destination for families and nature lovers, **PROSPECT PARK** in Brooklyn has lots to discover!

Stroll through **Long Meadow** and set up a picnic, say hi to the resident ducks and geese, try finding all seven playgrounds, and then explore the lush **Ravine**. Prospect Park is Brooklyn's backyard!

Home to the borough's only forest, the Ravine portion of the park
has a stream that runs through it *and* a secret waterfall!

Treat your four-legged friend with a trip to **Dog Beach**, where pooches
are allowed to doggy-paddle off-leash and run free in the grass!

Afterward, see how far your own paddling can take you as you glide
in one of the rental boats that float across **Prospect Park Lake**.

LET'S KEEP EXPLORING

To the subway we go! Turn to page 21.

There is no way better to travel the city than gliding across the water on the **NYC FERRY**!

The ferry is like a taxi that drives on water. It connects New Yorkers from the waterfront communities of the Bronx, Brooklyn, Manhattan, and Queens through multiple stops along the river.

Be sure to watch for the ferry's name as you board. The fleet was named by New York City schoolchildren, who voted for their favorite. Names include *Lunchbox*, *Seas the Day*, and *Friendship Express*. Which name do you like best?

The horn blows loud and off we go! Climb up the stairs to the ferry's rooftop for a breezy ride and views of the city skyline.

WHERE TO NEXT?

Head to the beach! Turn to page **24**.
Craving delicious dumplings? Turn to page **26**. ⟶

Want to get there super-fast?
Head down to the **SUBWAY** tracks!

New York's underground train system connects neighborhoods throughout the city, and it's the most convenient way for people to get where they want to go.

Did you know that if you lined up all the subway tracks, they would stretch over **600 miles**? (That's the distance from New York City to Chicago!)

WHERE TO NEXT?

Carnival rides and treats! Turn to page **22**.
Snack time! Let's get some cannolis! Turn to page **28**.

UPTOWN

Three miles of sandy beaches, countless rides, and New York's only aquarium can all be found at the city's playtime destination: **CONEY ISLAND!**

Coney Island is considered the birthplace of the American amusement park and modern roller coaster. The first park here opened its doors way back in the early 1800s.

Today, Coney Island is still home to the legendary (wooden!) **Cyclone roller coaster**, go-karts, a retro Ferris wheel, sideshow performances, and multiple theme-park thrills. But there's more to see than just amusements . . .

Don't miss the world's most famous eating contest—the fastest hot-dog eaters on the planet compete for the prestigious honor of winning the **Mustard Belt**. It's a Fourth of July experience that's hard to digest!

How many hot dogs do you think you could eat in 10 minutes?

All this contest talk is making me hungry...

WHERE TO NEXT?

Want to sample yummy dumplings? Turn to page **26**. Or fresh ravioli? Turn to page **28**.

Surf's up! Let's catch a wave in Far Rockaway!

ROCKAWAY BEACH is the largest urban beach in the United States. Nicknamed **Rockapulco**, this famous Queens beach is frequented by surfers. It's the only place in the five boroughs where you can hang ten and legally catch a wave.

The beach is **7 miles long** and offers plenty of sand for your towel and making castles.

No sun? No problem! Rockaway Beach also offers playgrounds, spots for fishing, and areas for basketball games and sandy volleyball.

WHERE TO NEXT?

Eager to try dragon fruit and green tea ice cream? Turn to page **26**.

Hankering for pasta and cream-filled cannoli? Turn to page **28**.

Festivals and parades, incredible parks, temples, and community markets— a visit here is like taking a trip to China without a plane ticket!

CHINATOWN is one of the most vibrant neighborhoods in Manhattan, and it's the ultimate foodie destination. Watch talented chefs create hand-pulled noodles from scratch, try some crispy Peking duck, or slurp on soup dumplings. Don't forget dessert! Egg cake, please! Or maybe dragon bread?

New York's most colorful celebration is the **Chinese New Year Festival**, which marks the start of spring and the beginning of a new year on the Chinese calendar. The streets are filled with joyful parades, exploding firecrackers, dragon dancers, and confetti everywhere.

WHERE TO NEXT?

What's up around the corner?
Turn to page **30**.
Let's walk a little farther north!
Turn to page **32**.

Ciao, **LITTLE ITALY!**
This Lower Manhattan neighborhood
is known for its Italian roots—
and lots of delicious eats!

Italian Immigrants moved to this area
of New York in the 1800s, bringing
along their language and customs.

Grab a table on the sidewalk to enjoy savory meatballs and spaghetti or a perfectly melted panini on the go. End with a creamy cannoli and sweet gelato!

One of the city's oldest street fairs is the **Festival of San Gennaro**, a week-long celebration in September that honors the patron saint of Naples. Thousands of vendors set up booths, and there's live music and plenty of carnival rides and games.

WHERE TO NEXT?

Let's turn here on this street! Turn to page **30**.
This way—there's another neighborhood to see!
Turn to page **32**.

Uh-oh, we followed the smells of delicious food and now we're lost . . .

Is this the same neighborhood?!

The avenues run north to south, right?

And the streets run east to west.

Wait . . . weren't Manhattan's streets built in the shape of a grid?

What does it mean when
my map looks like this?

WHICH WAY SHOULD WE GO?

This way? Turn to page 26.
That way? Turn to page 28.
Or over there? Turn to page 32.

Let's take a stroll through the heart of **GREENWICH VILLAGE**, a stomping ground for bohemians and artists!

The Village is known for its charming brownstones, one of which is designated as New York City's smallest home. It's only **9 ½ feet wide**!

Checkmate! Are you ready to play? The southwest corner of **Washington Square Park** is a battleground . . . for chess! Try your hand at a game with one of the locals.

A giant marble sculpture—the **Washington Square Arch**—welcomes visitors to the park. The arch is one of the most recognizable monuments in the city and has long been a popular gathering spot for artists and performances. Do you hear that piano playing?

Feel free to jump into the fountain to cool off! The park's large stone fountain is one of the only ones in the city that you're allowed to splash in.

WHERE TO NEXT?

Get lost in book stacks! Turn to page **34**.

Visit a park built on train tracks! Turn to page **37**.

New York's favorite literary nook, **THE STRAND**, is home to over 18 miles of books (and counting!).

You can literally get lost in the stacks at the Strand, a legendary destination for an amazing collection of new, used, and rare books. There are over **2½ million books** for sale!

From classic children's titles to the latest releases—and even a whole floor dedicated to rare and first editions—the Strand is a book lover's dream.

Want to hear a story? The kids' story-time sessions are often visited by costumed characters. What book character would you like to meet in person?

MAKE TRACKS!

The subway gets you around fast!
Turn to page 50.

Want to take a bite out of the Big Apple?
Head to the Meatpacking District's famous food hall:
CHELSEA MARKET!

Chelsea Market is so big that it takes up an entire block. Inside, you can find some of the best food counters, bakeries, and restaurants in the city, all under one roof.

Many people don't know that this building has a sweet history: the famous Oreo cookie was invented right here! Chelsea Market is housed within the original facility of the National Biscuit Company, which later became **Nabisco**.

Look above the market and you'll see a park up in the sky!

The **HIGH LINE** is a public park built on a historic freight rail line.

Watch your step! The High Line designers incorporated the original train tracks into the park. You can also find a miniature forest, a grassy area for lounging, and a splash pad!

ONWARD! Continue your adventurous day on the subway! Turn to page **50**.

The **NEW YORK PUBLIC LIBRARY** holds many stories and treasures, and it is loyally guarded by Patience and Fortitude, the marble lions at the entrance!

When you have some serious reading to do, head to the majestic **Rose Main Reading Room** on the top floor. Reference books line the shelves, and visitors read under murals of billowing clouds and blue sky above.

The Map Room is a fun stop for explorers. Twirl the main globe a few times to find . . .

Wait—where did New York go? I don't see it on the globe!

New York City has (literally) been wiped off the map by all the people who have touched its spot when they visited!

WHERE TO NEXT?

Take a grand terminal tour! Turn to page 40.
Visit an out-of-this-world park! Turn to page 44.

All aboard to GRAND CENTRAL STATION!

If you want to see stars, look up! Grand Central's celestial ceiling features a constellation of zodiac signs painted in gold leaf, plus over **50 stars** illuminated by glittering LED lights. Can you find Orion?

YOUR TRAIN IS ABOUT TO DEPART! WHERE ARE YOU HEADED?

To a home-run stadium! Board on page **46**.

To a wild animal encounter! Board on page **56**.

To try soul food! Board on page **58**.

Or how about a stroll on Fifth Avenue? Walk over to page **54**.

Want to see the bustling center of NYC?
42ND STREET, TIMES SQUARE
is the place to be!

Here you will find bright city lights, enormous billboards, and talented street performers—even a famous cowboy singing in his underwear!

Climb to the top of the TKTS stadium seating to catch the action, high above the ground and the rushing traffic below.

WHERE TO NEXT?

Time for a curtain call!
Turn to page **52**.
A grand station to explore!
Turn to page **40**.

The Unisphere is a beloved symbol of Queens—
it's the world's largest globe structure and
CORONA PARK's centerpiece!

The stainless steel model of Earth was originally built for the **1964 New York world's fair** to celebrate humankind's achievements in space travel.

Do you think the planet looks like it's floating? It was designed to!

A racket of fun surrounds the structure, including a small zoo, a science museum, and the **Arthur Ashe Stadium**, which hosts the U.S. Open tennis tournament every year.

WHERE TO NEXT?

Rock on over to a beach adventure! Turn to page **24**.
Explore a grand concourse! Turn to page **40**.

Nothing says New York like a visit to **YANKEE STADIUM**—home to the baseball world champions!

Bright lights and bleacher seats . . .

Is there anything better than seeing a home run by the home team?

Ruth, DiMaggio, Gehrig, Mantle, Jeter . . .

So many baseball greats have worn the pinstriped uniform.

WHERE TO NEXT?   A special park that lights the way! Turn to page **60**.
Hail a taxi from the game! Turn to page **48**.

TAXI TIME—let's look for a ride!
Watch for a yellow car with a number on
top. When it shines bright, it's available!

The first New York City taxis were painted red and green. The color was changed in the 1960s, after a study found that bright yellow was most noticeable from a distance.

If you could choose any color for the taxis, what would it be?

WHERE TO NEXT?

Head to Fifth Avenue for a stroll! Turn to page **54**.
Explore Central Park's castle! Turn to page **65**.

Metrocard swipe and a double beep,
Into the tunnel we go deep!

You'll find more than just trains on the **SUBWAY** platforms. Many stations are underground art galleries, decorated with colorful glass mosaics that tell stories about the neighborhood above them. At the **14th Street station**, you'll find fun art sculptures of peculiar creatures. Can you spot one?

Hop on the train, but make sure to wait for passengers to exit first!

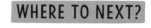

WHERE TO NEXT?

Say hi to New York's famous lions! Turn to page **38**.
Visit New York's largest intersection! Turn to page **42**.

The world-renowned **THEATER DISTRICT** dazzles visitors with live shows and performances.

Did you know that **Broadway** was the first street in NYC to be fully illuminated by electric lighting?

In 1880, this section of the city was so bright from billboards and theater lights that it gained the nickname "**The Great White Way**."

Today, the area is known as the Theater District, but there's so much more to see! The streets burst with neon signs, flashy billboards, and gourmet restaurants offering a variety of delicious cuisines!

Find your seats and get settled in.

Lights down, curtains up—the show is about to begin!

WHERE TO NEXT?

See a starry sky inside. Turn to page 40.

Try some tasty street cart snacks!
Turn to page 54.

No faster way to grab something to eat,
than from NYC's food cart elite!

How could you resist so many enticing sidewalk smells?
From chicken kebabs to gyros, candied nuts to halal—
the **5TH AVENUE** food carts have yummy cuisines from all
over the globe. Don't forget New York's famous salty pretzel, too!

WHERE TO NEXT?

A dino-mite adventure awaits!
Turn to page 62.

Watch puppets dance on stage!
Turn to page 64.

Ready for an animal adventure? The **BRONX ZOO** is one of the largest wildlife conservation parks in America!

This urban jungle is known for its diverse animal collection—you can see more than **600 species** from around the globe. Visit with the animals of an Asian jungle, the African plains, and Himalayan highlands. Get up close with a gorilla in the Congo Gorilla Forest, or say hello to the big cats at Tiger Mountain.

The zoo houses over **6,000** animals, including giraffes, bears, and sea lions, plus a children's zoo where you can meet and greet farmyard friends.

After you're done visiting the animals, bug out on the zoo's **Bug Carousel**. Don't worry, these critters don't crawl or bite. They're carved from wood and painted to resemble real life. It's the first and only carousel in the world dedicated to insects!

MORE FUN AHEAD!

Animal adventures continue! Turn to page **62**.

Jazz music with a
side of soul food?
Take the A Train—
to **HARLEM**, we go!

Harlem is the perfect place to visit when you want to connect with music.
Live jazz, gospel, and hip-hop spill into the streets from the many clubs, restaurants, and churches.

Feeling hungry? World-famous BBQ ribs and fried chicken, potato salad, mac and cheese, creamy collard greens—and don't forget the cornbread! Nothing's better than terrific soul food to fill your belly.

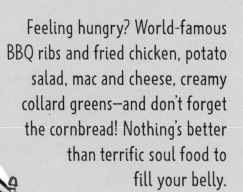

WHERE TO NEXT?

Visit the house that Ruth built!
Turn to page **46**.

Explore an old lighthouse!
Turn to page **60**.

Next to the **GEORGE WASHINGTON BRIDGE** and right on the **Hudson River** stands the last remaining lighthouse in **Manhattan**.

¡MANGOS!

The Little Red Lighthouse is a special New York gem. It has become widely known as a literary landmark due to the popular children's book *The Little Red Lighthouse and the Great Gray Bridge.*

The lighthouse opens its doors just one fall day per year, allowing visitors to climb the spiral staircase and take in the view. The festival celebrates the lighthouse with readings, fishing clinics, art, live music, and activities for all ages.

SO MUCH MORE TO SEE!

Head back downtown by taxi! Turn to page **48**.

Ready to let out a roar? Let's go explore!

THE AMERICAN MUSEUM OF NATURAL HISTORY

contains over **33 million** cultural objects and is one of the most visited museums on the planet!

It has the largest collection of dinosaur bones in the world, including a **Titanosaur**—one of the biggest species ever found. The fossil is so massive that the head and part of the neck stick out of the gallery, welcoming visitors off the elevators.

THE TITANOSAUR

Have a whale of a time with another big attraction! The **94-foot-long blue whale** is also a famous museum resident. The model whale weighs **21,000 pounds** and hangs only by its dorsal fin, appearing to magically swim through the air.

WHERE TO NEXT?

Take in a charming theater show! Turn to page **64**.
Row, row, row to the heart of Central Park! Turn to page **66**.

Wooden figurines come alive and dance with strings at this charming theater hidden among **CENTRAL PARK**'s trees.

Talented puppeteers perform tales of pirates, princesses, and giants at the **Swedish Cottage Marionette Theater** to the delight of enchanted audiences. Marionettes dance across the stage. Strings move up, strings move down, left to pirouette, and then tilt to take a bow!

Did you know that Central Park has its own castle?

The whimsical **Belvedere Castle** was built in 1869 to provide visitors with the best views of Central Park. (The name is fitting—it translates to "beautiful view" in Italian!) The castle has two balconies and a narrow spiral staircase made of stone. Don't forget to sit on the throne!

WHERE TO NEXT?

Have a boatload of fun!
Turn to page **66**.

Hail a taxi to Midtown!
Turn to page **68**.

Row, row, row your boat to the heart of New York's CENTRAL PARK!

At the **Loeb Boathouse**, visitors can rent an aluminum boat and go on a tour of The Lake. Dip under the historic **Bow Bridge** and take in a view of **Bethesda Fountain and Terrace** from the water's edge. Here you can watch bubble magicians and other street performers, which often include opera singers practicing their vocals.

There's no shortage of nature to see in **The Lake**. Be sure to look out for the turtle and duck residents!

THE SUN IS STARTING TO SET!

Better hail a taxi, quick! Turn to page 68.

Wait for a yellow taxicab to come near,
One hand in the air so it can spot us here!
TAXI, TAXI!

Maybe we should whistle?

One last stop to visit the king
of the New York City skyline: the
EMPIRE STATE BUILDING!

Soaring **1,454 feet above Manhattan**, the Empire
State Building is one of the world's tallest
skyscrapers and New York City's most iconic
structure.

Climbing to the top of the **102nd-floor
observation deck** offers a spectacular view.
All of the city's neighboring states
and boroughs magically twinkle
in front of you.

EMPIRE STATE

We gaze out over the Big Apple as the sun gently sets on a big city adventure we'll never forget.

ADVENTURE INDEX

Want to learn even more about New York City? We've compiled fun facts, history, and helpful hints about favorite locations to help you explore further during your city journey! Make sure to check the websites with an adult for up-to-date information before your visit.

STATUE OF LIBERTY Pages 2-3

Did you notice that the crown has 7 rays? Not just a lucky number, 7 represents the number of the world's continents, and each ray weighs over 150 pounds. If you are hoping to climb to the top of the Statue of Liberty's crown, act fast! Crown tickets often sell out 6 months in advance. **Liberty Island, New York Harbor · nps.gov**

Nearby Adventures

THE STATUE OF LIBERTY MUSEUM Get up close to the original torch and see a life-size replica of the Statue of Liberty's foot (seriously!) at this incredible, state-of-the art museum located next to the statue on Liberty Island. **Liberty Island, New York Harbor · statueofliberty.org**

SEAGLASS CAROUSEL Ride "underwater" on this magical fish-themed carousel in Battery Park, just steps from the Statue of Liberty Ferry landing. Tip: The fish glow with opalescence come sundown, making it a great night time swim as well. **State Street at Pearl Street, Battery Park, Manhattan · seaglasscarousel.nyc**

CASTLE CLINTON Tour a circular fortress in Battery Park that once functioned as the first immigration station for New York. During the summer, the fortress becomes a backdrop for free theater shows and plays! **South Battery Park, Manhattan · nps.gov/cacl/index.htm**

STATEN ISLAND FERRY
Pages 4-5

The ferry dates back to the 1700s and is one of the country's oldest transportation services. Today it's one of the busiest, with over 22 million riders annually. The free ride takes about 25 minutes, just enough time to settle into a window seat. The ferry runs 24 hours a day, 7 days a week. **Whitehall Terminal, 4 Whitehall Street, Manhattan · siferry.com**

Nearby Adventures

STATEN ISLAND ZOO Did you know that Staten Island Chuck boasts a higher accuracy rating than his rival, Punxsutawney Phil? You can visit the famous furry meteorologist at his bungalow at the Staten Island Zoo, along with other animal friends, year round. **614 Broadway, Staten Island · NYstatenislandzoo.org**

STATEN ISLAND YANKEES Cheer on the hometown minor league baseball team, the Staten Island Yankees! The stadium offers fun family-themed events, firework celebrations, and skyline views of Manhattan. **75 Richmond Terrace, Staten Island · milb.com/staten-island**

SNUG HARBOR CULTURAL CENTER While touring this urban oasis, be sure to visit the Chinese Scholar's Garden, where you can watch koi fish in the pools and relax with waterfalls. **1000 Richmond Terrace, Staten Island · snug-harbor.org**

DELI/BAGEL

Bagels made their way to NYC with the migration of Jewish immigrants in the late 1800s. Bagel production started in small, privately owned bakeries, and by 1900 over seventy bakeries existed in Manhattan's Lower East Side neighborhood. Today bagels can be found at countless grocery stores, bakeries and delis across the city. Here are a few of the most famous:

RUSS AND DAUGHTERS New York's premier Jewish deli has been located on the Lower East Side for over 100 years. Stop by and try a bagel with smoked salmon and lox on top, their specialty. **179 East Houston Street, Manhattan** · **russanddaughters.com**

ESS-A-BAGEL Crowds line up around the block for these bagels, long considered the best in New York City. **831 3rd Avenue, Manhattan** · **ess-a-bagel.com**

THE BAGEL STORE Here you can find creative and colorful bagel versions made popular by social media. The technicolor "Rainbow" is the most famous. Don't forget the funfetti flavored cream cheese! **69 5th Avenue, Brooklyn** · **NYthebagelstoreonline. com**

BROOKLYN BRIDGE

Heads up! The elevated walkway over the bridge is 1.3 miles long and open to both pedestrians and cyclists. Practice caution during your visit, and remember this rhyme: pedal to the left, step to the right. Carefully watch that center line! Cyclists are known to speed through as if they were in a road race.

MANHATTAN SIDE The Seaport District is a short walk from the bridge entrance! Located directly on the East River, this historic neighborhood holds treasures such as Bowne & Co. Stationers, as well as The South Street Seaport Museum and its fleet of ships to explore! **seaportdistrict.nyc**

BROOKLYN SIDE Walk down to the riverfront to visit Jane's Carousel, which is a few blocks from the bridge pedestrian entrance in Brooklyn. Dip into the park's Main Street Playground, and then grab a pie to go from one of the many neighborhood pizza restaurants. **brooklynbridgepark.org**

LOWER MANHATTAN: WORLD TRADE CENTER

The World Trade Center was deliberately constructed at a height of 1,776 feet, to honor the signing of the Declaration of Independence in the year 1776. It is the tallest building in the United States! The One World Observatory, located on the 100th-102nd floors, gives visitors an incredible view of the city. **285 Fulton Street, Manhattan** · **oneworldobservatory.com**

Nearby Adventures

9/11 MEMORIAL AND MUSEUM Located at the former location of the Twin Towers, the 9/11 Memorial and Museum commemorates the September 11, 2001, attacks. The memorial pools are free and open to the public. **180 Greenwich Street, Manhattan** · **911memorial.org**

CHARGING BULL Designed by an artist after the collapse of the stock market in the 1980s, the Charging Bull is a symbol of hope and strength for Wall Street. Visitors come from across the world to rub his nose and horns (and one other body part) for good luck. **Broadway at Morris Street, Manhattan**

NEW YORK STOCK EXCHANGE Did you hear that bell? That means it's time for the New York Stock Exchange to buy and sell! Billions and billions of stocks are traded daily here, the epicenter of the financial market. **11 Wall Street, Manhattan** · **nyse.com**

FEDERAL HALL NATIONAL MEMORIAL A giant statue of George Washington watches over Wall Street at Federal Hall, a National Memorial that is adjacent to the Stock Exchange. It is here where the Bill of Rights was born and George took the first president's oath over 200 years ago. **26 Wall Street, Manhattan** · **federalhall.org**

DUMBO, BROOKLYN: JANE'S CAROUSEL & WASHINGTON STREET

A name that is a fun acronym (which stands for Down Under the Manhattan Bridge Overpass) this popular neighborhood is known for its waterfront park, yummy restaurants, and the best views of the Manhattan skyline.

Nearby Adventures

BROOKLYN BRIDGE PARK Wander through the 85-acre riverfront oasis that stretches 1.3 miles across Brooklyn. The park contains multiple playgrounds, a carousel, sports facilities, and even a roller rink! **334 Furman Street, Brooklyn · brooklynbridgepark.org**

PEBBLE BEACH Skip over to Pebble Beach, a rocky shoreline along the East River for waterfront exploring and pebble throwing. **Brooklyn Bridge Park at Main Street, Brooklyn**

WASHINGTON STREET Snap a pic at the Instagram-famous view where the Manhattan Bridge is framed perfectly between buildings on a cobblestone street. The Empire State Building peeks through the bridge base! **Washington Street between Front Street & Water Street, Brooklyn**

DUMBO, BROOKLYN: PIZZA Pages 14-15

There are many pizzerias in DUMBO that vie for the best pie in the city. The fight has raged on for years, and the competition is fierce . . . which is your favorite?

GRIMALDI'S Grimaldi's pizzeria is one of the oldest pizzerias in NYC and known for their "secret recipe" dough. **1 Front Street, Brooklyn · grimaldispizzeria.com**

JULIANA'S Juliana's was opened by one of the original Grimaldi's founders, Patsy Grimaldi, creating a fierce competitor for Grimaldi's. **19 Old Fulton Street, Brooklyn · julianaspizza.com**

IGNAZIO'S Ignazio's is known for their famous pizza recipe dubbed simply "The Pizza." **4 Water Street, Brooklyn · ignaziospizza.nyc**

Other Famous Slices in the City

LOMBARDI'S Taste a slice of history! This historic pizzeria is credited with developing "New York Style" pizza and is the first pizzeria in the United States. **32 Spring Street, Manhattan · firstpizza.com**

JOHN'S OF BLEECKER STREET Known to fans as John's Pizza, this historic pizzeria was founded in 1929 and serves coal-fired brick-oven pizza to long lines of devoted fans. **278 Bleecker Street, Manhattan · johnsbrickovenpizza.com**

BROOKLYN HEIGHTS, BROOKLYN: NY TRANSIT MUSEUM Pages 16-17

All aboard the New York Transit Museum, the largest museum in the United States devoted to urban transportation history! During the holidays the museum takes its trains on a run through the city, allowing the public to ride back in time on the museum's vintage fleet. **99 Schermerhorn Street, Brooklyn · nytransitmuseum.org**

Nearby Adventures

JUNIORS CHEESECAKE Take a bite of world famous cheesecake at Junior's! This iconic diner has a full food menu of deli staples, too. **386 Flatbush Avenue, Brooklyn · juniorscheesecake.com**

BROOKLYN HEIGHTS PROMENADE Take a stroll on the pedestrian walkway that has an amazing view of Lower Manhattan. **Remsen Street to Orange Street along the East River, Brooklyn**

BROOKLYN BRIDGE PARK ROLLER SKATING RINK Roll on over to Pier 2 in Brooklyn Bridge Park. The covered pavilion offers roller skating sessions and rentals for all ages. **Pier 2, Brooklyn Bridge Park, Brooklyn · brooklynbridgepark.org/activities/roller-skating**

PARK SLOPE, BROOKLYN: PROSPECT PARK Pages 18-19

Prospect Park is Brooklyn's backyard! The sprawling urban oasis has over 585 acres of woodlands, waterways, and trails to explore and countless activities and recreation.

Nearby Adventures

PEDAL BOATS + KAYAK RENTALS Head over to Lakeside at the LeFrak Center and rent a pedal boat or kayak to take out on Brooklyn's only lake. **171 East Drive, Prospect Park, Brooklyn · lakesidebrooklyn.com**

PROSPECT PARK ZOO See over 600 animals at the Prospect Park Zoo, including sea lions, pandas, and baboons. **450 Flatbush Avenue, Brooklyn • prospectparkzoo.com**

PROSPECT PARK CAROUSEL Spin on over to the Prospect Park Carousel, located right outside the zoo entrance, to ride on one of the 54 colorful horses. **95 Prospect Park West, Prospect Park, Brooklyn • prospectpark.org**

GRAND ARMY PLAZA The arch in Grand Army Plaza was designed to mimic the Arc de Triomphe in Paris, France. The plaza under the arch is the location for many events—don't miss the large and lively farmers market! **1 Grand Army Plaza, Brooklyn**

FERRY Page 20

One of the most scenic ways to travel in the city is the NYC ferry! It's the same price as a MetroCard swipe (and young children travel free), allowing for commuters and tourists alike to explore NYC by the waterways. A few fun ferry stops to add to your next adventure:

BEST FERRY STOP FOR FUN IN THE SUN: ROCKAWAY BEACH The NYC ferry connects Lower Manhattan and Sunset Park, Brooklyn, to Rockaway Beach—allowing eager beachgoers direct access to sun, surf, and sand in less than an hour.

BEST FERRY STOP FOR A LIBRARY: LONG ISLAND CITY This Queens stop will put you steps from the state-of-the-art Hunters Point Library. Be sure to visit the outdoor reading garden surrounded by trees and take in the city view from the library's windows!

BEST FERRY STOP FOR A PLAYGROUND: SOUTH WILLIAMS-BURG Walk a few blocks from this Brooklyn stop to one of the most unique playgrounds in the city—Domino Park! Built on the site of the former Domino Sugar Refinery, the waterfront playground's design was inspired by the steps of the sugar refining process.

BEST FERRY STOP FOR FOODIES: DUMBO Steps from the ferry exit you'll have numerous restaurants competing for your attention—including some of the best pizzerias in the city. Top off the meal with ice cream from the historic fireboat house, right on the waterfront.

SUBWAY Page 21

Four Fun Facts about the Subway System!

LOTS OF TRACKS If you laid all the subway tracks end to end, they would stretch over 660 miles, That's the distance from New York City to Chicago!

SUBWAY GLOBES The green or red globes at many subway entrances have a special meaning. Entrances with red globes are closed at night, while those with green globes are open 24 hours a day.

ABOVEGROUND Many think the subway is only underground in New York City—which is false! Only 60 percent of the subway system is underground; the rest is aboveground with amazing window views.

SECRET STOP Shhhh! Did you know that there is a secret subway stop? City Hall station was abandoned in 1945, but it can still be viewed today by in-the-know riders of the 6 train. Stay on board at the final stop in Lower Manhattan as the train loops back around to go uptown—the secret City Hall station can be seen by looking through the windows!

CONEY ISLAND, BROOKLYN
Pages 22-23

Made famous by the historic amusement parks and a lively boardwalk, there's much to see during a visit to Coney Island. The best part: it's easy to access by subway train! The D-F-N-Q trains all stop here (and are just steps away from the beach!).

Nearby Adventures

LUNA PARK This amusement park offers modern rides, roller coasters, games, and an arcade and is home to the historic (and wooden!) Cyclone roller coaster. **1000 Surf Avenue, Brooklyn • lunaparknyc.com**

DENO'S WONDERLAND Deno's features adult rides plus a separate amusement park with rides for young children. The main attraction is the Wonder Wheel, a 150-foot Ferris wheel built in 1920 with cages that swing back and forth while in motion. **3059 West 12th Street, Brooklyn • denoswonderwheel.com**

NEW YORK AQUARIUM New York City's only aquarium is located right off the beach on Coney Island's celebrated boardwalk. Don't miss *Ocean Wonders: Sharks!*, an exhibit that holds more than 500,000 gallons of water and plenty of dorsal fins! **602 Surf Avenue, Brooklyn • nyaquarium.com**

NATHAN'S FAMOUS There's no better place to have a hot dog than the original, iconic location of Nathan's Famous in Coney Island. Don't miss the Hot Dog Eating Championship countdown clock located on the side of the building! **1310 Surf Avenue, Brooklyn • nathansfamous.com**

ROCKAWAY BEACH, QUEENS
Pages 24-25

Much more than just sand and crashing waves, Rockaway Beach offers a variety of playgrounds and other outdoor activities:

SURFS UP! Head over to the beachfront at 87th-91st Streets to see hundreds of surfers try to catch a wave on one of New York's only surfing beaches. **nycgovparks.org/parks/rockaway-beach-and-boardwalk**

PLAYGROUNDS Swing over to one of the playgrounds when you need a break from the sand. Located right off the boardwalk, the 30th Street playground has an awesome water feature to help cool down after the hot sun. **Boardwalk between Beach 29th and Beach 30th Streets, Rockaway Beach, Queens**

ROCKAWAY BEACH SURF CLUB: Located a few blocks off the beach, this hip taco stand and patio is surrounded by colorful surfboard lockers and has good music and the yummiest tacos around. **302 Beach 87th Street, Rockaway Beach, Queens • rockawaybeachsurfclub.com**

CHINATOWN Pages 26-27

A bustling neighborhood that is home to the largest population of Chinese people in the Western Hemisphere, Chinatown has busy sidewalks packed with souvenir stores, spices, and fresh food markets. A few spots to discover during your neighborhood adventure:

MUSEUM OF CHINESE IN AMERICA (MOCA) Learn about the history, heritage, and culture of Chinese immigrants at the Museum of Chinese in America, and take part in their family activities, such as calligraphy classes. **215 Centre Street, Manhattan • mocanyc.org**

CHINATOWN FAIR FAMILY FUN CENTER Get your game on at this legendary arcade that has classic favorites, such as air hockey, Skee-Ball, basketball, car racing, and ticketed prize games. **8 Mott Street, Manhattan • chinatownfair.biz**

THE ORIGINAL CHINATOWN ICE CREAM FACTORY Grab a cone at this family-owned ice cream factory that is famous for adding yummy Chinese-influenced ingredients to their ice cream, such as red bean, durian and lychee! **65 Bayard Street, Manhattan • chinatownicecreamfactory.com**

LITTLE ITALY Pages 28-29

Little Italy is packed full of history, incredible street art and delicious places to eat! A few to discover during your neighborhood adventure:

FERRARA BAKERY & CAFE Stop for a dessert break at Ferrara Bakery & Cafe to try their sweet cannolis and other Italian delicacies. This historic cafe has been a Little Italy staple since 1892. **195 Grand Street, Manhattan • ferraranyc.com**

FEAST OF SAN GENNARO FESTIVAL Every year since 1926, the streets of Little Italy are taken over by celebrations, performances, rides, games, and processions. The festival runs for 10 days in mid-September and draws large crowds from across the globe. Don't miss the cannoli-eating contest! **sangennaronyc.org**

FIRST STREET CULTURAL PARK Wander through First Street Cultural Park, an open-air art park that showcases contemporary artists—just a few blocks outside of Little Italy. The park is known to have some of the best graffiti in the city. **33 East 1st Street, Manhattan**

WE'RE LOST! Pages 30-31

Did you know that New York City's streets have hidden directional clues to help you explore the city? Here's a few facts and tips, so you don't get lost again!

STREETS AND AVENUES Above Houston Street, Manhattan is primarily a grid! Here there are two kinds of roads: streets and avenues. Avenues run north to south, and streets run east to west.

NAMED STREETS South of Houston Street (and some in the Meatpacking District/Village area) have names instead of numbers. These streets are the oldest in Manhattan and were originally created around popular walking routes and livestock paths. As the city grew, the twisting streets became confusing, so the city adopted a structured grid in 1811.

GOING THE DISTANCE City blocks vary in size and are generally much longer between avenues and shorter between streets. Twenty city blocks (measuring north to south) are equivalent to 1 mile.

CENTRAL LINE Fifth Avenue is Manhattan's central dividing line. Streets running east of 5th Avenue are titled "East" (i.e., East 46th St), and streets to its west are titled "West."

BROWN STREET SIGNS Street name signs with brown backgrounds are in areas that are officially designated as historic districts by the New York City Landmarks Preservation Commission.

GREENWICH VILLAGE Pages 32-33

The heart of Greenwich Village is Washington Square Park. With two playgrounds, a fountain that you can splash in, and even a dog park for your four-legged friend, Washington Square Park will hit the mark for a fun family afternoon. After a park visit, try these nearby adventures:

CHESS DISTRICT Checkmate! A short walk from Washington Square Park is the unofficial "Chess District," which includes a few stores that are devoted solely to the game that sell boards, games and anything else you may need to play. **Thompson Street between West 3rd Street and Bleecker Street, Manhattan**

SMALLEST HOUSE Visit the narrowest house in the city! It was built in 1873 and measures only 9 feet, 6 inches wide. **75½ Bedford Street, Manhattan**

STONEWALL INN After the riots in 1969, Stonewall Inn became the center of New York's LGBTQ+ rights movement. Visit the Inn and Stonewall National Monument that sits in the neighboring park, and stroll across the rainbow street crosswalk that has been painted across Christopher Street. **Stonewall Inn. 53 Christopher Street, Manhattan · thestonewallinnnyc.com**

MURRAY'S CHEESE Say cheese! Murray's, the oldest cheese shop in NYC, opened in Greenwich Village in 1940. Stop in their flagship store to try a sample, or grab a sandwich or cheese plate on the go. **254 Bleecker Street, Manhattan · murrayscheese.com**

STRAND BOOK STORE Pages 34-35

Boasting "18 miles of books and counting" the Strand has a mammoth collection of more than 2 million books on 4 floors. Don't miss the second-floor children's corner, book discount bins, and weekly author readings and book presentations. **828 Broadway, Manhattan · strandbooks.com**

Nearby Adventures

MAX BRENNER CHOCOLATE BAR & RESTAURANT Tubular lines pump chocolate along the ceiling at this chocolate factory, restaurant, and yummy desert palace. A sweet stop for all ages. **841 Broadway, Manhattan · maxbrenner.com**

UNION SQUARE PARK Home to a large bustling playground, dog park, and plenty of shaded benches, Union Square is a popular gathering place famous for its lively farmers market that features over 100 vendors. **East 14th Street to East 17th Street, Manhattan · unionsquarenyc.org**

NEW YORK COSTUMES Play dress-up at New York Costumes, a giant year-round costume and accessory superstore that is an entire city block long and encompasses two (packed to the ceiling!) floors. **104 4th Avenue, Manhattan · newyorkcostumes.com**

HIGH LINE & CHELSEA MARKET
Pages 36-37

While eating your way through the halls of Chelsea Market, don't miss the many artifacts from the original Nabisco factory! Near the main entrance on 9th Avenue there is a small display showcasing memorabilia from the original factory. There are also two murals located in the middle of the market, one of which is of an Oreo cookie. **75 9th Avenue, Manhattan · chelseamarket.com**

THE HIGH LINE Explore a park built in the sky on a historic rail line! Walk two stories above the buildings, take in the art installations, and stop to try some food from local vendors. Don't miss the High Line's outdoor theater seating that overlooks 10th Avenue—a fun way to view the city! **Gansevoort Street to 34th Street, along 10th to 12th Avenues, Manhattan · thehighline.org**

Nearby Adventures

CHELSEA PIERS Learn, practice, and play over 25 different sports at the massive complex that offers classes as well as day passes. **62 Chelsea Piers, Manhattan · chelseapiers.com**

PIER 62 CAROUSEL + SKATE PARK Twirl on over to the Hudson River Park's Pier 62 Carousel featuring 33 hand-carved wood figures that depict native Hudson River Valley animals. Next door is a popular skate park. **West 22nd Street and Hudson River, Manhattan · hudsonriverpark.org/locations/pier-62**

THE WHITNEY MUSEUM OF AMERICAN ART Explore multiple floors and art-filled outdoor balconies to learn about 19th- and 20th-century American artists including Jackson Pollock, Jeff Koons, Andy Warhol, and Georgia O'Keeffe. Don't miss the open studio for families on Saturdays and Sundays! **99 Gansevoort Street, Manhattan · whitney.org**

NY PUBLIC LIBRARY Pages 38-39

In the Children's Room of the NY Public Library you'll find some familiar friends: Winnie the Pooh, Piglet, Tigger, and Eeyore! These stuffed animals belonged to the real-life Christopher Robin. **476 5th Avenue, Manhattan · nypl.org**

Nearby Adventures

BRYANT PARK The NY Public Library's backyard is home to many events, including ice skating in the winter and popular movie nights in the summer. The park also hosts free activities including board games rentals, ping-pong tables, juggling lessons, and magic shows. **40th and 42nd Streets & 5th and 6th Avenues, Manhattan · bryantpark.org/programs#kids**

OUTDOOR READING ROOMS Read in the shade of the canopy trees at Bryant Park's popular outdoor reading rooms, where you can wander through shelves of books, newspapers, and magazines and borrow the material to read while visiting the park. **40th and 42nd Streets & Fifth and Sixth Avenues, Bryant Park, Manhattan**

BRYANT PARK FOUNTAIN Visit the granite fountain that is famously known to freeze in the winter, creating a frosty art piece. **41st Street & 6th Avenue, Bryant Park, Manhattan · bryantpark.org**

LE CARROUSEL Catch a ride on this merry-go-round in French classical style that features 14 animals (including a whimsical frog, a cat, a deer, and a rabbit) and spins to French cabaret music. You may just think you are in Paris! **Near 40th Street in Bryant Park, Manhattan · bryantpark.org**

BRYANT PARK BATHROOMS Bryant Park is home to something quite unique . . . a special bathroom! Funded by private donors, the elegant bathrooms have fresh flowers, artwork on the walls, full time attendants, and ambient classical music. **Located near 42nd Street, Bryant Park East, Manhattan**

GRAND CENTRAL STATION

Pages 40-41

Need to find your friends in the busy train station? Meet them under the clock! Not only is it an information booth with agents to help with train schedules and ticketing, the golden clock and information kiosk is the busiest gathering spot in the city. **Main Concourse, Grand Central Station, Manhattan**

Nearby Adventures

NEW YORK TRANSIT MUSEUM GALLERY ANNEX AND STORE All aboard! A small outpost of the Transit Museum in Brooklyn is located in Grand Central Station. The Annex houses a transit-oriented gift shop as well as a space for exhibitions, and is also the home to the popular (and free!) Holiday Train Show. **Grand Central Terminal (42nd Street and Park Avenue), Manhattan · nytransitmuseum.org/visit**

WHISPERING GALLERY Shhhhh! The ceramic arches of the lower terminal pathway in Grand Central Station creates an acoustical phenomenon that is known as the whispering gallery. Grab a friend and stand diagonally apart, in opposite corners, while leaning toward the wall. A soft whisper will be heard loud and clear, as if you're standing directly next to each other! **Grand Central Terminal (42nd Street and Park Avenue), Manhattan · grandcentralterminal.com/what-to-see**

UNITED NATIONS A short walk from Grand Central Station is the official headquarters of the United Nations. Overlooking the East River, this sprawling complex offers various tours when not in session. **760 United Nations Plaza, Manhattan · visit.un.org**

TIMES SQUARE 42ND STREET

Pages 42-43

Stretching from West 42nd to West 47th Streets, Times Square is known as "the crossroads of the road" as it's a major intersection, bustling tourist haven, and entertainment destination for New Yorkers and visitors alike.

Nearby Adventures

TIMES SQUARE NEW YEARS EVE BALL High above 42nd Street is the glittering New Year's Eve attraction—the Times Square Ball! Located on the roof of One Times Square, the crystal-encrusted ball descends down a special flagpole at 11:59 p.m. on New Year's Eve to grand fanfare. **One Times Square, Manhattan · timessquarenyc.org**

TKTS STEPS Step right up for a prime view of Times Square! The TKTS booth in Times Square was built with rooftop bleacher seats, offering an amazing view of one of the world's busiest intersections. **Father Duffy Square, Broadway and 47th Street, Manhattan · tdf.org/nyc/7/TKTS-ticket-booths**

M&M'S WORLD TIMES SQUARE Wander through rainbow-coated floors at this fun store dedicated to the popular chocolates. **1600 Broadway, Manhattan · mms.com**

MIDTOWN COMICS Explore this super-powered comics institution that has the largest selection of comic books, graphic novels, and action figures in the city. **200 West 40th Street, Manhattan · midtowncomics.com**

QUEENS: FLUSHING MEADOWS CORONA PARK Pages 44-45

As the largest Park in Queens, Flushing Meadows-Corona Park has lakes, scenic trails, museums and even a zoo. A few to discover on your next visit:

U.S. OPEN - ARTHUR ASHE STADIUM Serve up some fun at Arthur Ashe Stadium. Part of the USTA Billie Jean King National

Tennis Center, it is the main stadium of the US Open tennis tournament in August and the largest tennis stadium in the world. **14 Meadow Corona Park, Flushing, Queens • usopen.org**

NEW YORK HALL OF SCIENCE Explore this hands-on science center with over 450 interactive exhibits including the space-themed Rocket Park Mini Golf and the award-winning 60,000-square-foot Science Playground. **47–01 111th Street, Corona, Queens • nysci.org**

QUEENS ZOO Small but charming, this 18-acre zoo in the middle of Corona Park has a large variety of animals and a fun farmyard for kids. **53-51 111th Street Corona, Queens • queenszoo.com**

YANKEE STADIUM Pages 46-47

Let's play ball! Yankee Stadium is more than just an NYC attraction—it is a destination for baseball fans all across the world. A few things not to miss during your visit:

MONUMENT PARK II Be sure to catch Monument Park II, an open-air museum where you can see the retired Yankees numbers and read a bit about players' history. **Yankee Stadium, Bronx • mlb.com/yankees**

THE NEW YORK YANKEES MUSEUM Get a home run of history at this sports museum located inside Yankee Stadium, featuring memorabilia and a "Ball Wall" centerpiece, a collection of autographs of current and former Yankees. **Yankee Stadium, Bronx • mlb.com/yankees**

KIDS CLUBHOUSE Shaped like a mini-baseball field, this playground has larger-than-life baseballs, bats, and peanut climbing apparatuses along with slides and activities for the youngest of Yankees fans. **Yankee Stadium, Bronx • mlb.com/yankees**

TAXI Pages 48-49

Five Fun Facts about NYC's Yellow Cabs!

1. New York City has more than 13,000 yellow taxis.

2. Each taxi makes nearly 800 trips per month.

3. Do all taxi cabs match? Yes! There is a "Taxi Cab Yellow" color. It is Dupont M6284, to be exact.

4. New York City cabbies attend class for 40 hours before becoming a certified driver and must purchase a medallion number before operating a vehicle.

5. Hold on to your phone and camera! Over 35% of the items reported lost in the backseat of a taxi cab are electronics.

SUBWAY Pages 50-51

Best Subway Art That's Worth a Stop

NYC has some of the best museums in the world—but did you know that some of the most unique art is underground? Here are a few of the best art installations that can be found in the NYC Subway System:

72nd Street Station: B and C Trains

SKY Yoko Ono designed the gorgeous mosaics that depict a blue sky filled with white puffy clouds, bringing a bit of the outdoors to the indoor subway platform.

14th Street/Eighth Avenue Station: A, C, E, and L Trains

LIFE UNDERGROUND Keep your eyes peeled to see artist Tom Otterness's adorable bronze figurines that are playfully hiding on railings, benches, and ceiling beams through the station.

59th Street-Columbus Circle; 1, A, C, B, and D Trains

WHIRLS AND TWIRLS This large colorful tile installation by Sol Lewitt makes it feel as if you are walking into a rainbow at the Columbus Circle Station.

THEATER DISTRICT Pages 52-53

A wonderful way to experience NYC's culture is to have a night out at the theater! Most of the city's theaters are located in the Theater District in Midtown Manhattan, alongside many top restaurants and other places of entertainment. Here's a look at some of the experiences:

BROADWAY SHOW NYC has nearly 40 theaters in the district—with a wide variety of shows, plays musicals, and adaptations for all ages. Family favorites include *Lion King*, *Aladdin*, and *Wicked*. For discounted shows, head to a TKTS booth, where you can get last-minute tickets up to 50% off. **Multiple locations, including a large booth "under the steps" in Times Square. Father Duffy Square at Broadway and 47th Street, Manhattan • tdf.org/nyc/8/Locations-Hours**

NEW VICTORY THEATER Take in a children's show at the New Victory Theater—New York City's first (and only!) full-time cultural performing theater for kids. **209 West 42nd Street, Manhattan • newvictory.org**

CARMINE'S Enjoy an Italian feast at Carmine's, where all menu items are served family style. The portions are overly generous—come hungry! Reservations essential. **200 West 44th Street, Manhattan • carminesnyc.com**

ELLEN'S STARDUST DINER Watch talented waiters sing and dance along with show tunes while you enjoy a meal at Ellen's Stardust Diner, the only restaurant with a singing waitstaff in the city. **1650 Broadway, Manhattan • ellensstardustdiner.com**

5TH AVENUE/STREET FOOD
Pages 54-55

Fifth Avenue has long been considered a top retail district in the city and one of the most famous shopping districts in the world! Be sure not to miss these iconic shopping destinations and unique experiences during your visit:

LEGO STORE See Rockefeller Center in miniature! Visit the Lego Store to see Rockefeller Center built out of Lego bricks and to do some Lego kit shopping. This store carries Lego pieces specific to New York. **620 5th Avenue, Manhattan • rockefellercenter.com/shops/lego**

FAO SCHWARZ Costumed toy soldiers greet guests at the door at this legendary toy store that is known for its unique toy selection, larger-than-life plush animals, and fun in-store demonstrations. Don't miss the opportunity to dance on the famous *Big* piano! **30 Rockefeller Plaza, Manhattan • faoschwarz.com**

FDNY FIRE ZONE Learn about fire safety at the FDNY Fire Zone, a fire-safety learning center with interactive exhibits, including fire demonstrations and an on-site fire truck. **61 West 48th Street, Manhattan • fdnysmart.org/firezone**

TOP OF THE ROCK Visit Top of the Rock Observation Deck for a top view of New York! The indoor and outdoor platforms offer the best views of the city. **30 Rockefeller Plaza, Manhattan • topoftherock.com**

MOMA Marvel at modern art and installations at the world-famous museum. Be sure to check out the awesome art tours! **11 West 53rd Street, Manhattan • moma.org**

BRONX ZOO
Pages 56-57

After visiting the animals, swing over to the Bronx Zoo's Tree Top Adventures where you can embark on a wild rope and bridge course through the tall trees and bushes. The zoo also offers a thrilling zipline adventure over the Bronx River. **2300 Southern Boulevard, Bronx · bronxzoo.com**

NEW YORK BOTANICAL GARDEN Relax on the gorgeous grounds, explore the Children's Adventure Garden, and tour the Edible Academy where you can learn about foods and help grow (and pick) fruits and vegetables. **2900 Southern Boulevard, Bronx · nybg.org**

WAVE HILL Tour the beautiful public garden and cultural center, and join in Wave Hill's weekend family art projects or popular nature-themed weekends. **4900 Independence Avenue, Bronx · wavehill.org**

EDGAR ALLAN POE COTTAGE Visit the historic former home of the American writer and poet Edgar Allan Poe. **2640 Grand Concourse, Manhattan · bronxhistoricalsociety.org/poe-cottage**

HARLEM Pages 58-59

Vibrant and culturally diverse, Harlem is a neighborhood known for its music and delicious food. During your visit, check out the names of the streets and avenues; many of them have been after civil rights leaders, such as Malcolm X Boulevard and Martin Luther King Jr. Boulevard.

APOLLO THEATER Do you have a special talent or love to sing? Register for the long-running, live, weekly talent competition on the world-famous Apollo Theater stage. Amateur Night at the Apollo Auditions are open to singers, dancers, comedians and variety artists ages 5 and older. **253 West 125th Street, Manhattan · apollotheater.org**

HARLEM MEER Named after the Dutch word for "lake," the Meer is a large body of water in Central Park. Be sure to catch the fun fishing programs during the summer. **106th–110th Streets, next to Dana Discovery Center, Central Park, Manhattan · centralparknyc.org/attractions/harlem-meer**

SOUL FOOD Fill your belly with collard greens, corn bread, bread pudding, and other soul food specialties at Sylvia's Restaurant. **328 Malcolm X Boulevard, Manhattan · sylviasrestaurant.com**

TOTALLY KIDS CAROUSEL Take a twirl on a unique carousel! A local artist designed Totally Kids Carousel based on children's drawings of animals. **Riverbank State Park, near 140th Street, Manhattan**

NATIONAL JAZZ MUSEUM IN HARLEM Get jazzy with some history at the National Jazz Museum in Harlem, where you can learn about amazing musicians and artists. **58 West 129th Street, Manhattan · jazzmuseuminharlem.org**

LITTLE RED LIGHTHOUSE Pages 60-61

After being slated for destruction, the lighthouse was saved thanks to thousands of children who loved Swift's book and started a nationwide campaign. Children are the reason it stands in Fort Washington to this day! **Fort Washington Park, Hudson River Greenway, Manhattan**

Nearby Adventures

FORT TRYON PARK Wander through the tree-lined paths of Fort Tryon Park, along the Hudson River. The annual autumn Medieval Festival in Fort Tryon Park is a family favorite. **Riverside Drive to Broadway, West 192nd Street to Dyckman Street · forttryonparktrust.org**

THE MET CLOISTERS Explore this outpost of the Metropolitan Museum of Art and marvel at their medieval paintings, incredible stained-glass windows, and tapestries. **99 Margaret Corbin Drive, Manhattan · metmuseum.org/visit/plan-your-visit/met-cloisters**

SUGAR HILL CHILDREN'S MUSEUM OF ART & STORYTELLING Create endless art in the studio or curl up with a book at the Sugar Hill Museum's Reading Nook at this museum that encourages creative thinking. **898 St. Nicholas Avenue at 155th Street, Manhattan · sugarhillmuseum.org**

AMERICAN MUSEUM OF NATURAL HISTORY Pages 62-63

Did you know that there is a special experience that allows you to fall asleep in the darkened halls of one of the world's most beloved museums? The Night at the Museum Experience allows you to search for fossils by flashlight and have a deep night's sleep under the famous blue whale. **200 Central Park West, Manhattan · amnh.org**

Nearby Adventures

PLATFORM EXHIBITS Be sure to stop at the subway station under the Natural History Museum—it is filled with special mosaics that represent the evolution of life. The various animals, sea creatures, and replicas of fossilized bones bring the museum underground, all for only a subway card swipe! **81st Street-Museum of Natural History (Manhattan, B, C Lines)**

PLANETARY WATERPARK During summer, the one-acre terrace outside the Rose Center for Earth and Space becomes an out of this world sprinkler pad for kids to splash and play. **American Museum of Natural History · 200 Central Park West, Manhattan · amnh.org**

NEW YORK HISTORICAL SOCIETY MUSEUM & LIBRARY In 1804, the New-York Historical Society opened as New York's first museum. Pay a visit to the Children's History Museum on the lower level, where interactive stations bring over 350 years of New York and American history to life. **170 Central Park West at 77th Street · nyhistory.org**

CENTRAL PARK WEST Pages 64-65

BELVEDERE CASTLE Belvedere Castle is NYC's meteorologist! In the early 1900s, the castle was made an official weather station for New York City. Look closely at the very top of the building— you can see the scientific instruments churning and working. **Mid-park at 79th Street · centralparknyc.org/attractions/belvedere-castle**

SWEDISH COTTAGE MARIONETTE THEATER Catch a puppet show at the charming Swedish Cottage Marionette Theater, set within the beautiful background of Central Park's foliage. Stick around after the show for a special behind-the-curtain experi-ence, where talented puppeteers show kids how strings make the puppets sing and dance. **Advance tickets required. Central Park at 79th Street · centralparknyc.org/attractions/swedish-cottage-marionette-theatre**

Nearby Adventures

HECKSCHER PLAYGROUND The oldest playground in Central Park is also one of the largest with more than 1.8 acres of play space and equipment, including a large sand area, a splashy water feature, and a rocky cliff for little climbers. **Mid-park around 63rd Street · centralpark.com/things-to-do/attractions/heckscher-playground**

STRAWBERRY FIELDS Walk through Strawberry Fields and pay respect to the Imagine mosaic, both of which are a tribute to John Lennon. **Right inside Central Park West between 71st and 74th Streets · centralpark.com/locations/strawberry-fields**

TURTLE POND Located next to Belvedere castle. You'll discover hundreds of turtles who call this magical pond home. **Mid-park at 79th Street, Manhattan · centralpark.com/things-to-do/attractions/turtle-pond**

CENTRAL PARK EAST Pages 66-67

BETHESDA TERRACE Wander through Bethesda Terrace where you can see the fountain, Bow Bridge, Loeb Boathouse, and numerous ducks and turtles all from the water's edge. Enjoy the free street performances on the mosaic terrace, which often include opera singers who love the amazing acoustics. It is also the favorite spot for many bubble artists, who will happily make a bubble the size of a person for a tip! **Mid-park at 72nd Street, Manhattan · centralparknyc.org/attractions/bethesda-terrace**

CENTRAL PARK ROW BOATS Grab an oar and explore Central Park's lake that spans over 22 acres! Row boats are available to rent by the half hour at the Loeb Boathouse, located adjacent to Bethesda Terrace. The fleet consists of 100 boats, each of which seats four people. Tip: The boats are first come, first serve and require a cash deposit. **Seasonal/weather permitting. Life jackets provided. East 72nd Street and Park Drive North · thecentralparkboathouse.com/boats.php**

Nearby Adventures

REMOTE CONTROL SAILBOATS Rent a model boat and sail the day away at the Conservatory Water. All boats are wind-powered and remote-controlled using the trim of the sail and the direction of the rudder. **Located on the east side of the Conservatory Water. Half hour rentals are available first come, first serve.** • centralpark.com/things-to-do/sports/model-sailboats

BALTO STATUE Give a hug to Balto, the bronzed statue honoring the famous canine who saved children by delivering medicine through a blizzard in Alaska. **Located west of East Drive and 67th Street and north of the zoo, Central Park** • centralparknyc .org/attractions/balto

HANS CHRISTIAN ANDERSEN STATUE Visit the Hans Christian Andersen Statue and his not-so-ugly duckling for free storytelling hour—it takes place at the foot of the statue on Saturdays at 11 a.m. throughout the summer. **Located on a raised plaza west of the Conservatory Water, near East 74th Drive** • centralpark. org/hans-christian-andersen

CENTRAL PARK ZOO Have an adventure exploring Central Park's Zoo and its wild residents. (Don't miss the penguins!) Afterward, catch a performance of the zoo's charming Delacorte Musical Clock. The bronze animals dance as the chimes play one of 32 nursery rhymes every half hour. **Zoo entrance requires a ticket. Clock performance is free/open to the public. East side of Central Park, near 64th Street and Fifth Avenue** • centralparkzoo.com

CHESS AND CHECKERS HOUSE Checkmate! Play a friendly game of chess or checkers at Central Park's Chess and Checkers House, which has 24 permanent tables with inlaid chess boards. Board rentals and supplies are free! **Mid-park, near 64th Street** • centralparknyc.org/attractions/chess-checkers-house

TAXI Pages 68-69

Tips and Tricks on How to Grab a Cab in NYC

AVAILABILITY An illuminated number on the rooftop of a taxi indicates that it is available. The light will be off if the driver is off duty or if they already have a passenger!

PASSENGERS Most cabs take up to four people. The fare is per ride, not per person—there is no extra charge for more than one passenger.

HAILING A TAXI To hail a cab, simply extend or wave your arm—and if you want, you can even whistle or shout "taxi!" loud!

COLOR INDICATORS The iconic yellow cabs can pick up or drop passengers anywhere. The newer apple-green cabs serve riders north of East 96th and West 110th Streets in Manhattan and throughout the outer boroughs—the Bronx, Brooklyn, Queens, and Staten Island.

TAXI STANDS Taxi cabs cruise the streets for fares 24 hours a day. With the exception of Grand Central Terminal, Port Authority, and Penn Station, there are no taxi stands in the city.

EMPIRE STATE BUILDING Page 70

Visit the Empire State Building's galleries to learn about the history of the iconic skyscraper. One of the galleries lets you get up close and personal with the "King" himself. Bring your camera! **Galleries included with any Observatory Ticket. 350 5th Avenue, Manhattan** • esbnyc.com

Nearby Adventures

HERALD SQUARE & MACY'S Head over to Herald Square at the intersection of Broadway and 34th Street to see the home of Macy's, the New York's largest department store that encompasses over 2.2 million square feet! **Intersection of Broadway, 6th Avenue, and 34th Street, Manhattan**

LITTLE KOREA While only a couple blocks long, Little Korea (also known as K-Town) is packed with vibrant Korean culture. Explore hundreds of restaurants and retail shops that line the streets, and be sure not to miss the cutting-edge karaoke. **West 32nd Street between 5th and 6th Avenues**

MADISON SQUARE GARDEN Also known as MSG or simply "The Garden," Madison Square Garden hosts the best sporting events and entertainment and is known as the world's most famous arena. **4 Penn Plaza, Manhattan** • msg.com/madison-square-garden